LAUGH OUT LOUD!

THE FUNNY FOOD JOKE BOOK

Sean Connolly and Kay Barnham

W
FRANKLIN WATTS
LONDON • SYDNEY

First published in 2012 by Franklin Watts

Copyright © 2012 Arcturus Publishing Limited

Franklin Watts
338 Euston Road
London
NW1 3BH

Franklin Watts Australia
Level 17/207 Kent Street, Sydney, NSW 2000

Produced by Arcturus Publishing Limited,
26/27 Bickels Yard, 151–153 Bermondsey Street, London SE1 3HA

Editor: Joe Harris
Illustrations: Adam Clay and Dynamo Design
Layout Design: Notion Design

A CIP catalogue record for this book is available from the British Library.

Dewey Decimal Classification Number: 818.6'02-dc23

ISBN: 978 1 4451 1491 0

Franklin Watts is a division of Hachette Children's Books, an Hachette UK company.
www.hachette.co.uk

Printed in China

SL001839EN
Supplier 03, Date 0512, Print Run 1961

CONTENTS

FUNNY FOOD

Why did the biscuit cry?
Because his mum had
been a wafer
so long.

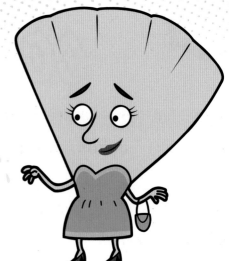

When do truck drivers stop for a snack?
When they see a fork in the road.

What did one plate say to the other plate?
Lunch is on me.

Knock knock.
Who's there?
Cash.
Cash who?
No, thanks. I prefer walnuts.

Why did the rhubarb go out with a prune?
Because he couldn't find a date.

FUNNY FOOD

This coffee is disgusting – it tastes like mud.
I'm not surprised – it was ground a few minutes ago!

Why did the chef serve frozen steak?
He wanted it to melt in the mouth.

What do you get if you cross a comedian and an orange?
Peels of laughter.

What do you call an aeroplane passenger covered in salt
and pepper?
A seasoned traveller.

What did the speedy tomato say to the slow tomato?
Ketchup!

FUNNY FOOD

What happened at the cannibals' wedding?
They toasted the bride and groom.

What cheese is made backwards?
Edam!

Why did the man eat yeast and furniture polish for breakfast?
He wanted to rise and shine.

Knock knock.
Who's there?
Arthur.
Arthur who?
Arthur any biscuits left?

How do you make a fruit punch?
Give it boxing lessons.

FUNNY FOOD

Why did the girl stare at the
orange juice carton?
Because it said 'concentrate' on
the label.

Why was the chef so
relaxed?
He had plenty of thyme
on his hands!

What's yellow and dangerous?
Shark-infested custard.

Waiter, waiter – there's a fly in my
soup!
Sorry, madam, I didn't know you
were vegetarian!

Did you hear about the turkey who tried to escape the
oven dish?
He was foiled.

FUNNY FOOD

What do you get if
you cross a
Shakespeare play
and an egg?
Omelette!

How do you know when a
cannibal feels like eating
you?
He keeps buttering you up!

What did the fat man say
when he sat down at the
dinner table?
'Just think – all this food is going to waist!'

How do you make gold soup?
Put 14 carrots in it!

What do you get if you divide the circumference of a
pumpkin by its diameter?
Pumpkin pi.

FUNNY FOOD

A pizza walks into a bar and asks for a lemonade.
'I'm sorry,' says the barman.
'We don't serve food.'

Chef: I didn't use a recipe for this casserole – I made it up out of my own head!
Customer: I thought it tasted of sawdust!

If I cut a potato in two, I have two halves. If I cut a potato in four, I have four quarters. What do I have if I cut a potato in sixteen?
Chips!

Why did the bakers work late?
Because they kneaded the dough!

How much did the pirate pay for his corn?
A buck an ear.

FUNNY FOOD

Waiter, can I have my lunch on the patio?
Certainly, sir, but most people find a plate more sensible!

Why should you never tell secrets in a corn field?
Because you would be surrounded by ears!

What farm animal can you spread on toast?
A baby goat – it's a little butter!

What's the most expensive item on the menu at a Chinese restaurant?
Fortune cookies.

Mmmmm! This cake is lovely and warm!
It should be; the cat's been sitting on it all afternoon!

FUNNY FOOD

What do computer
operators eat for a snack?
Chips!

How do they eat their chips?
One byte at a time.

Which snack is wicked and
lives in the desert?
The sand witch!

How do you keep flies out of
your kitchen?
Move the pile of rotting vegetables into the living room!

What starts and ends with 't', and is also full of 't'?
A teapot.

What kind of bird is at every meal?
A swallow.

FUNNY FOOD

Why did the vampire always carry a bottle of tomato ketchup?
He was a vegetarian!

What is the one thing that stays hot in the fridge?
Mustard!

What did the chewing gum say to the shoe?
I'm stuck on you.

Why did the tomato turn red?
Because he saw the salad dressing.

Knock knock.
Who's there?
Phil.
Phil who?
Phil this cup with sugar, would you, I've run out!

FUNNY FOOD

What do you get if you boil up 25 cars, three buses, and a truckload of sugar?
Traffic jam.

Why is cutting a slice of gingerbread the easiest job in the world?
It's a piece of cake.

What is the best time to pick apples?
When the farmer is away on holiday!

Customer: Why is there a dead fly in my soup?
Waiter: Well, you surely don't expect to get a live one at these prices!

What did one snowman say to the other snowman?
Smells like carrots.

FUNNY FOOD

Why did the man send his alphabet soup back?
Because he couldn't find words to describe it!

Did you hear about the farmer who took his cows to the North Pole?
He thought he would get ice cream!

Waiter – there's half a dead cockroach in my food!
You'll have to pay for the half you've eaten, sir!

How do you eat your Christmas turkey?
I just gobble it down!

Did you hear about the eggs who played tricks on people?
They were practical yolkers.

FUNNY FOOD

Why do bees have icky, sticky hair?
They use honeycombs.

Waiter – this crab only has one claw!
Sorry, sir, it must have been in a fight!
In that case, take it away and bring me the winner.

Doctor, I think I've just swallowed a chicken bone!
Are you choking?
No, I'm serious!

What do you call a lazy baker?
A loafer!

Waiter, this omelette tastes awful!
Sir, I can assure you that our chef has been making omelettes since he was a child!
That may be true, but can I have one of his fresher ones please?

FUNNY FOOD

Why did the lemon refuse to fight the orange?
Because it was yellow!

There's a stick insect in my salad – fetch me the branch manager at once!

Where is the best place to keep a pie?
Your tummy!

What type of lettuce did they serve on the Titanic?
Iceberg.

FUNNY FOOD

Did you hear about the paranoid potatoes?
They kept their eyes peeled for danger.

What do elves use to make sandwiches?
Shortbread!

Why are seagulls called seagulls?
Because if they flew over bays, they would be bagels.

What did the carrot stick say to the tortilla chip?
'Want to go for a dip?'

What sort of dog has no tail?
A hot dog!

FUNNY FOOD

What do rubbish collectors eat?
Junk food.

Teacher: Sally, give me a sentence with the word 'aroma' in it.
Sally: My uncle Fred is always travelling; he's aroma!

Teacher: Philip, why do you have a lunchbox in each hand?
Pupil: It's important to have a balanced diet, Mr Harrison!

What do you get if you mix birdseed with your breakfast cereal?
Shredded tweet.

What is worse than finding a worm in your apple?
Finding half a worm in your apple!

FUNNY FOOD

What's a cannibal's favourite takeaway?
Pizza with everyone on it.

What did the golfer eat for lunch?
A sand wedge.

Why are clocks greedy?
They always have seconds.

Why couldn't Batman go fishing?
Because Robin had eaten all the worms.

Did you hear about the strawberry who attended charm school?
He became a real smoothie.

Which part of Swiss cheese is the least fattening?
The holes!

FUNNY FOOD

What do you call a pig that does karate?
A pork chop.

Why did the potato cry?
Its peelings were hurt.

How do you make a stiff drink?
Put cement in your cup.

Did you hear about Professor Cole, the scientist who discovered the perfect ratio for mixing cabbage, carrot, onion and mayonnaise?
He called it Cole's Law.

Why did the girl disappear into the bowl of muesli?
A strong currant pulled her under.

FUNNY FOOD

Knock knock.
Who's there?
Police.
Police who?
Police can I have a chocolate milkshake?

What kind of nut always has a cold?
A cashew!

What do you call a fake noodle?
An impasta.

Johnny! How many more times do I have to tell you to keep away from the biscuit jar?
No more times – it's empty!

What do you get if you cross a chicken with a cement mixer?
A bricklayer.

FUNNY FOOD

Does Dracula's chef ever cook roast beef?
Yes, but very rarely.

What is a chicken's favourite dessert?
Layer cake!

Knock knock.
Who's there?
Anita.
Anita who?
Anita nother hot dog – I'm starving!

How do you fix a broken
pizza?
With tomato paste!

Why did the man
wear a
banana skin
on each foot?
He wanted a
pair of
slippers.

FUNNY FOOD

Our school lunches are untouched by
human hand – there's a gorilla in
the kitchen!

Why is a birthday cake
like a golf ball?
They both get
sliced.

Why are baked
beans and onions
dangerous?
Together they make tear gas.

Knock knock.
Who's there?
Army.
Army who?
Army and you still going for ice cream?

Waiter, do you serve crabs?
Of course, sir. We serve anybody.

FUNNY FOOD

Where do hamburgers dance?
At meatballs.

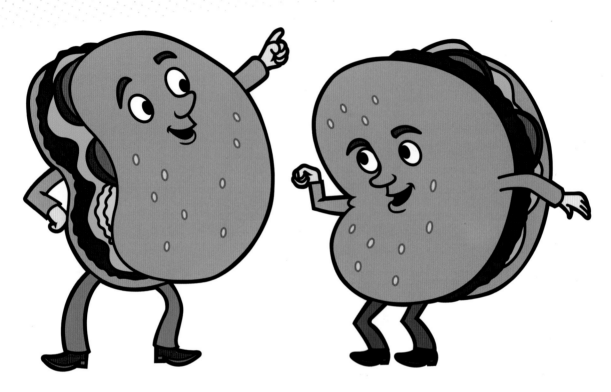

What is the frying pan's favourite song?
'Home on the Range.'

Why did the turkey cross the road?
It was the chicken's day off.

I'm on a seafood diet. The more I see food, the more I eat!

FUNNY FOOD

What did the grape say when someone trod on it?
It let out a little whine.

What did one strawberry say to the other?
'Look at the jam you've got us into!'

What do you call a woman with a nut tree on her head?
Hazel.

Why did Mrs Grape leave Mr Grape?
Because she was tired of raisin kids.

Waiter! There's a fly in my soup!
Yes, sir, it's the bad meat that attracts them.

What are apricots?
Where baby monkeys sleep.

FUNNY FOOD

We don't let Dad near the kitchen. The last time he cooked, he burned the salad!

Waiter, will my pizza be long?
No, it will be round.

What do you call
a cow with
three legs?
Lean beef.

What's the difference between a butcher and an insomniac?
One weighs a steak and the other stays awake.

What do you get from nervous cows?
Milkshakes!

FUNNY FOOD

What did one knife say to the other knife?
'Look sharp!'

Knock knock.
Who's there?
Wilma.
Wilma who?
**Wilma lunch
be ready
soon?**

**Did you hear the
joke about butter?**
I'm not telling you – you
might spread it.

**What did baby corn say to
Mummy corn?**
Where's popcorn?

What do you call stolen sweets?
Hot chocolate.

FUNNY FOOD

What do you get if you cross a turkey with an octopus?
Eight drumsticks for Christmas dinner.

Why did the man fill his waterbed with root beer?
Because he wanted a foam mattress.

Waiter, this food isn't fit for a pig.
I'm sorry sir; I'll bring you some that is.

What is a cannibal's favourite game?
Swallow the leader.

What do chimps wear when they're cooking?
Ape-rons!

FUNNY FOOD

What is lemonade?
When you help an elderly lemon cross the road.

Waiter – this food is terrible. Bring me the manager.
I'm sorry, sir. He won't eat it either.

You can eat dirt cheap at the local diner!
Maybe so, but who wants to eat dirt?

Waiter, there's a hand in my soup.
That's not your soup, sir, it's the finger bowl.

If it looks like a duck, walks like
a duck, and talks like a duck...
it probably needs a little
more time in the oven.

FUNNY FOOD

Why shouldn't you tell an egg a joke?
Because it might crack up!

What did the octopus hate about eating every night?
Washing his hands before dinner.

Which is the most musical fish?
The piano tuna.

Customer: Waiter, could you please tell me what I've just eaten?
Waiter: Why do you ask, sir?
Customer: Because I'll
need to tell the doctor
soon!

**Where do the
toughest,
meanest
chickens come
from?**
From hard-boiled
eggs.

FUNNY FOOD

If vegetarians eat vegetables, does that mean that humanitarians eat humans?

Waiter, waiter, have you smoked salmon?
No, sir, but I have smoked a pipe.

What does a billionaire make for dinner every night?
Reservations.

Waiter – is there soup on the menu?
No, sir. I wiped it off.

What do you call a man in a huge pot?
Stu.

Glossary

byte a measurement of information on a computer

circumference the distance around a circle

cockroach an insect with long legs and antennae

diameter the width of a circle

humanitarian someone who tries to keep people from suffering

insomniac someone who cannot sleep

paranoid worried that everyone wants to harm you

Further Reading

Blunt, Fred. *Belly Laughs: 150 Ribtickling Food Jokes.* Kingfisher, 2008.

Bozzo, Linda. *Food Jokes to Tickle Your Funny Bone.* Enslow Elementary, 2011.

Winter, Judy A. *Jokes About Food.* Raintree, 2010.

Index

Websites

CBBC 'Crack a Joke' game: *www.bbc.co.uk/cbbc/shows/cbbc-jokes*

Jokes by Kids website: *www.jokesbykids.com*

Yahoo! Kids Jokes: *http://kids.yahoo.com/jokes*